KT-497-735

Contents

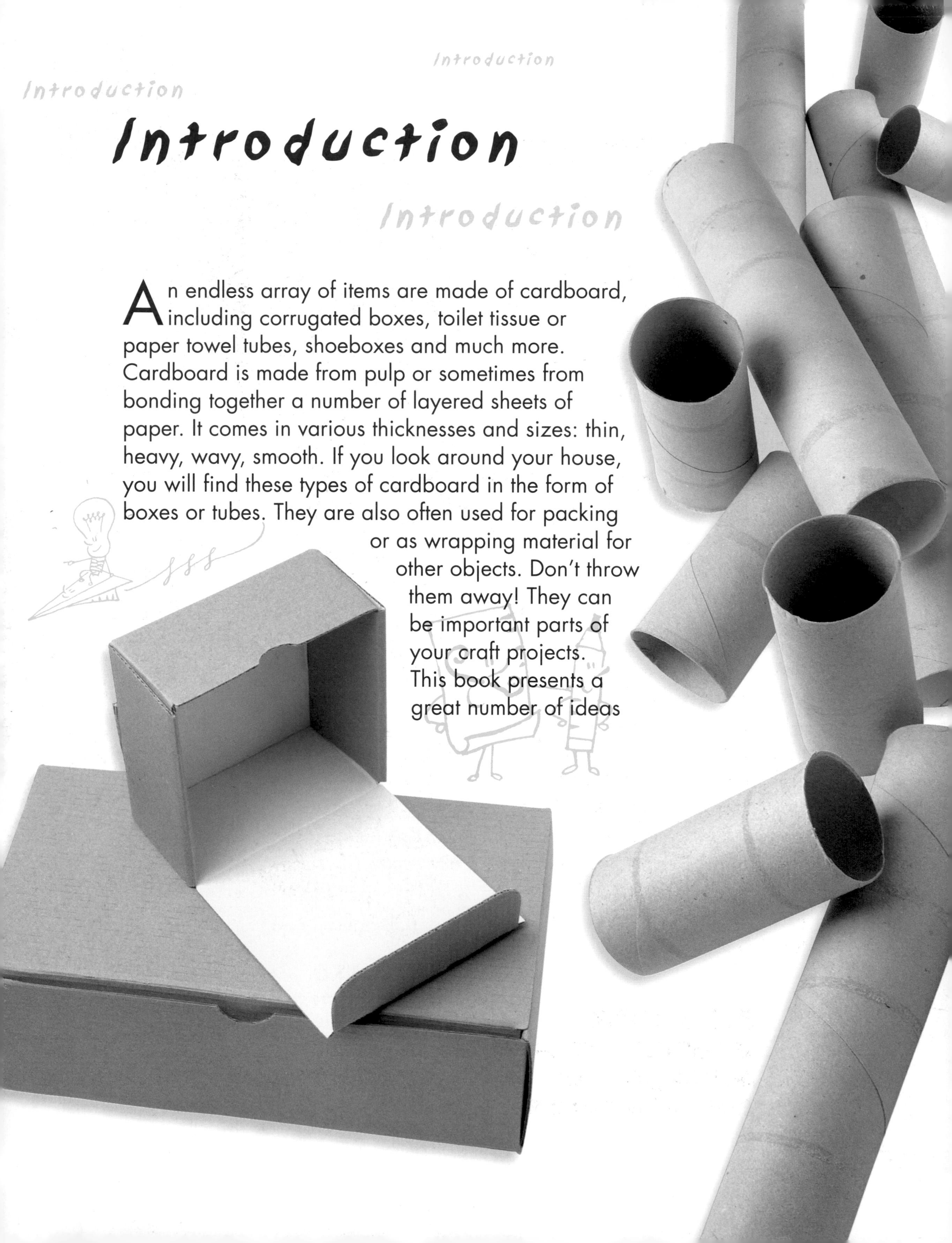

Introduction

Introduction

Introduction

Introduction

An endless array of items are made of cardboard, including corrugated boxes, toilet tissue or paper towel tubes, shoeboxes and much more. Cardboard is made from pulp or sometimes from bonding together a number of layered sheets of paper. It comes in various thicknesses and sizes: thin, heavy, wavy, smooth. If you look around your house, you will find these types of cardboard in the form of boxes or tubes. They are also often used for packing or as wrapping material for other objects. Don't throw them away! They can be important parts of your craft projects. This book presents a great number of ideas

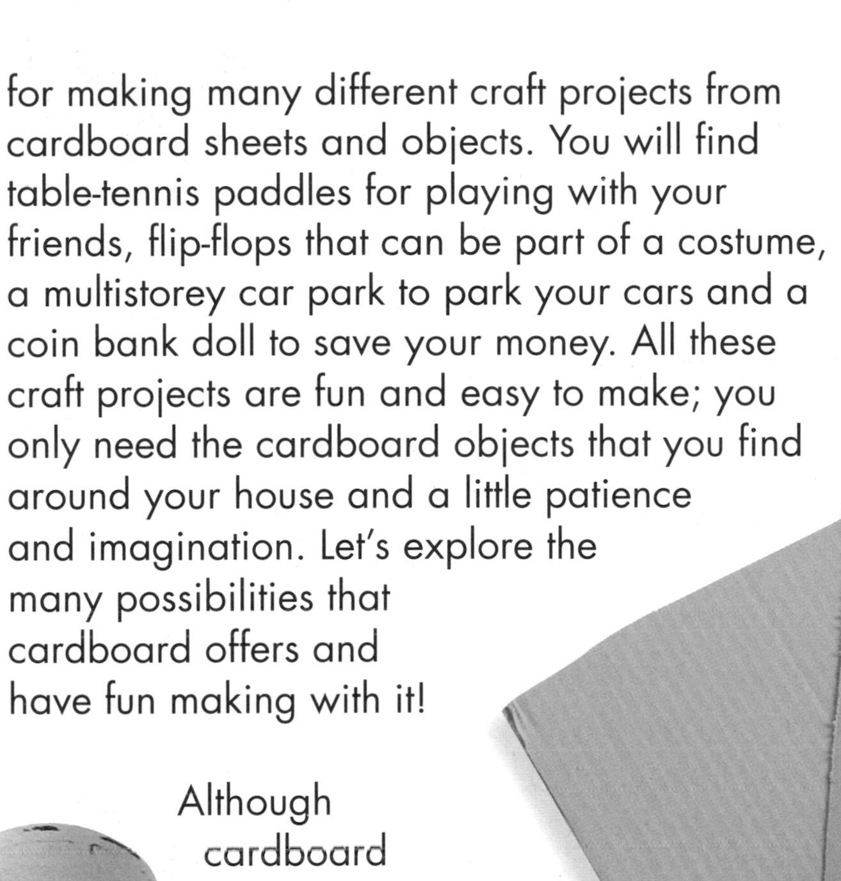

for making many different craft projects from cardboard sheets and objects. You will find table-tennis paddles for playing with your friends, flip-flops that can be part of a costume, a multistorey car park to park your cars and a coin bank doll to save your money. All these craft projects are fun and easy to make; you only need the cardboard objects that you find around your house and a little patience and imagination. Let's explore the many possibilities that cardboard offers and have fun making with it!

Although cardboard comes in many colours, you will notice that here we have chosen to use brown cardboard. This will allow you to paint it with your favourite colours and so make your projects more personal and creative. To make these projects you will need to have some basic items that are easily found at home (scissors, staples, glue...) and then follow the steps carefully.

REMEMBER!
Whenever you see this symbol, or when you are using scissors, ask an adult to help you.

Table-tennis Paddle

There's no need to buy paddles to play table-tennis. You can make them yourself by following these steps.

Toolbox

You will need:
- **thick, smooth cardboard**
- **black tape**
- **scissors**
- **glue**
- **white and pink paint**
- **foam pad**
- **felt-tip pen**
- **paintbrush**
- **ruler**

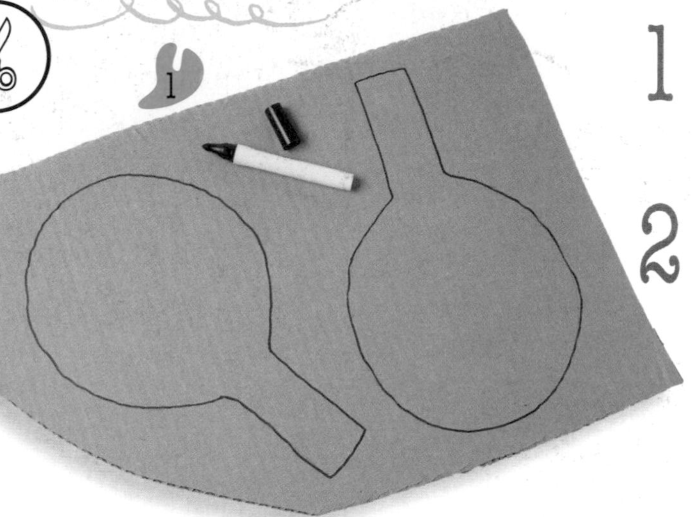

1 Draw and cut out two table-tennis paddles on a piece of thick, smooth cardboard.

2 Using one of the cut out paddles as a pattern, draw and cut out two circles and two handles. The cut out circles should have flat bases.

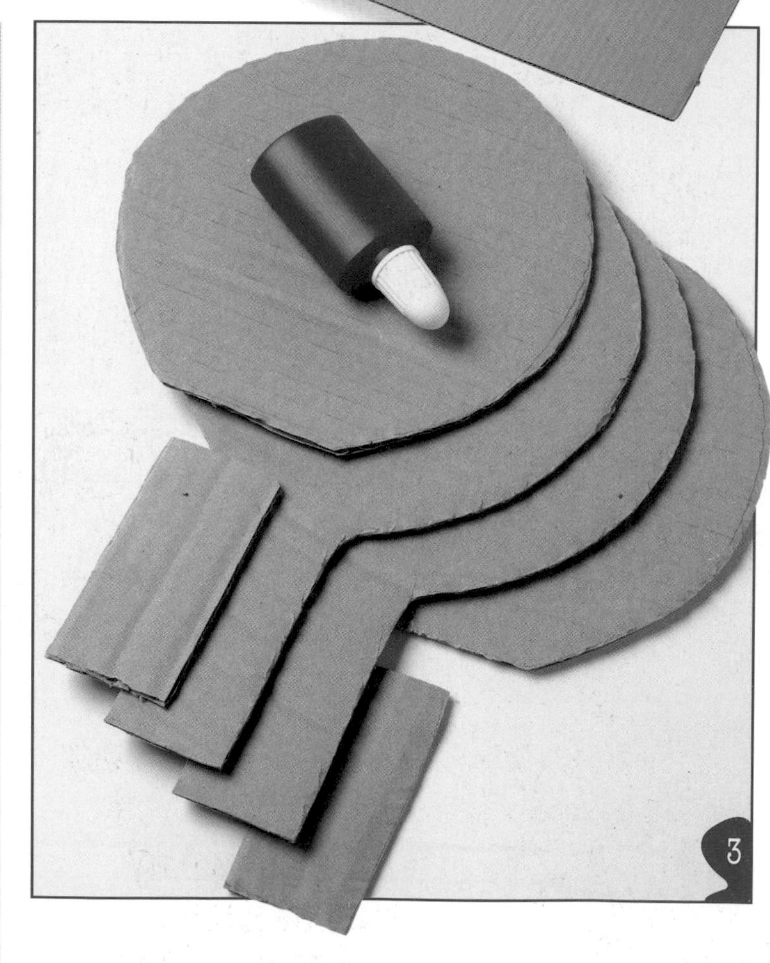

3 Glue the two paddles together. Then attach the circles and the two handles to each side of the paddle with glue.

4 Wrap the handle with black tape and paint both circles white.

5 When the white paint is dry, paint it pink using a foam pad.

Here is your paddle! Now you can play a great game of table-tennis!

Let your imagination soar

Other ideas:
You can create original paddles with different shapes, for example, a hand.

Snail

It is very easy to make a snail with two strips of cardboard. To bring it to life follow these step-by-step instructions.

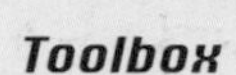

Toolbox

You will need:
- thin, corrugated cardboard
- thin, smooth cardboard
- scissors and clothes pegs
- glue
- orange, green, white, blue and red paint
- paintbrush
- felt-tip pen

1 Draw the body of the snail on a thin, smooth piece of cardboard and cut it out.

2 Cut out a strip of thin, corrugated cardboard about 15 cm long and 3 cm wide and paint orange stripes on it. This will be the shell of your snail.

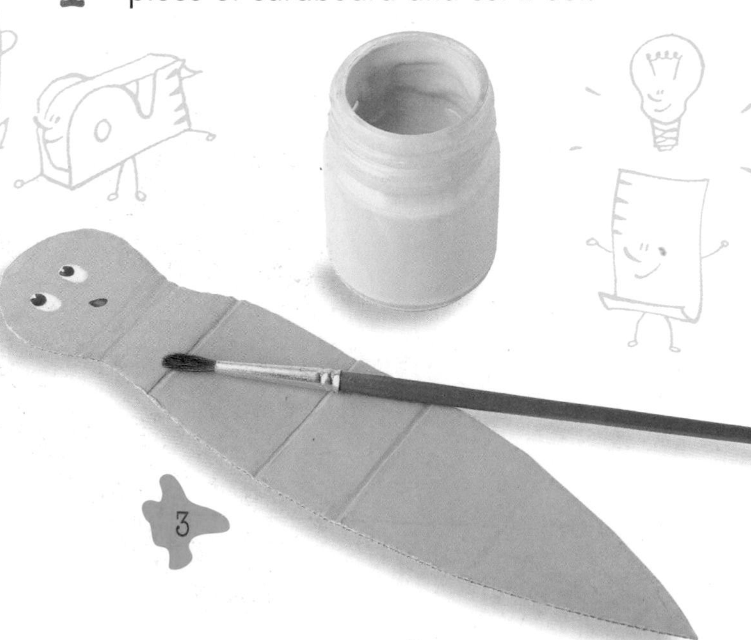

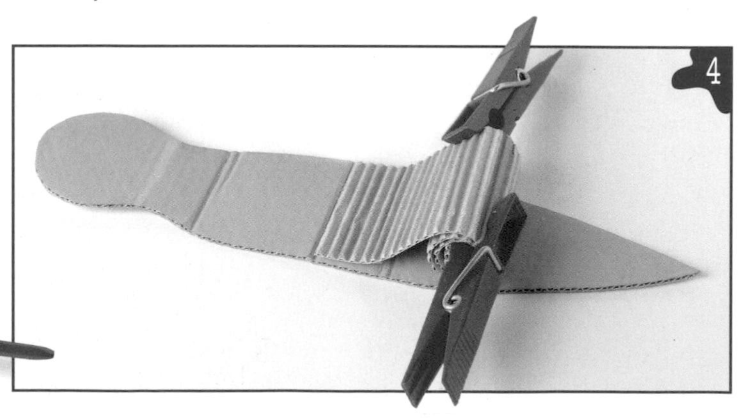

3 Paint the body green and when it dries paint the eyes and the mouth of the snail.

4 Glue one of the ends of the strip to the body to make the shell. Roll it and hold it in place for a while using two clothes pegs. This way, when you let it go it will keep its spiral shape.

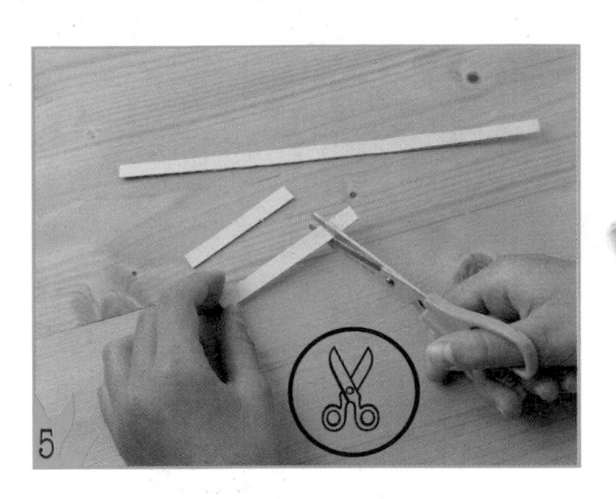

5 Cut out two strips approximately 4 cm long and 0.5 cm wide from a piece of thin, corrugated cardboard to form the antennae.

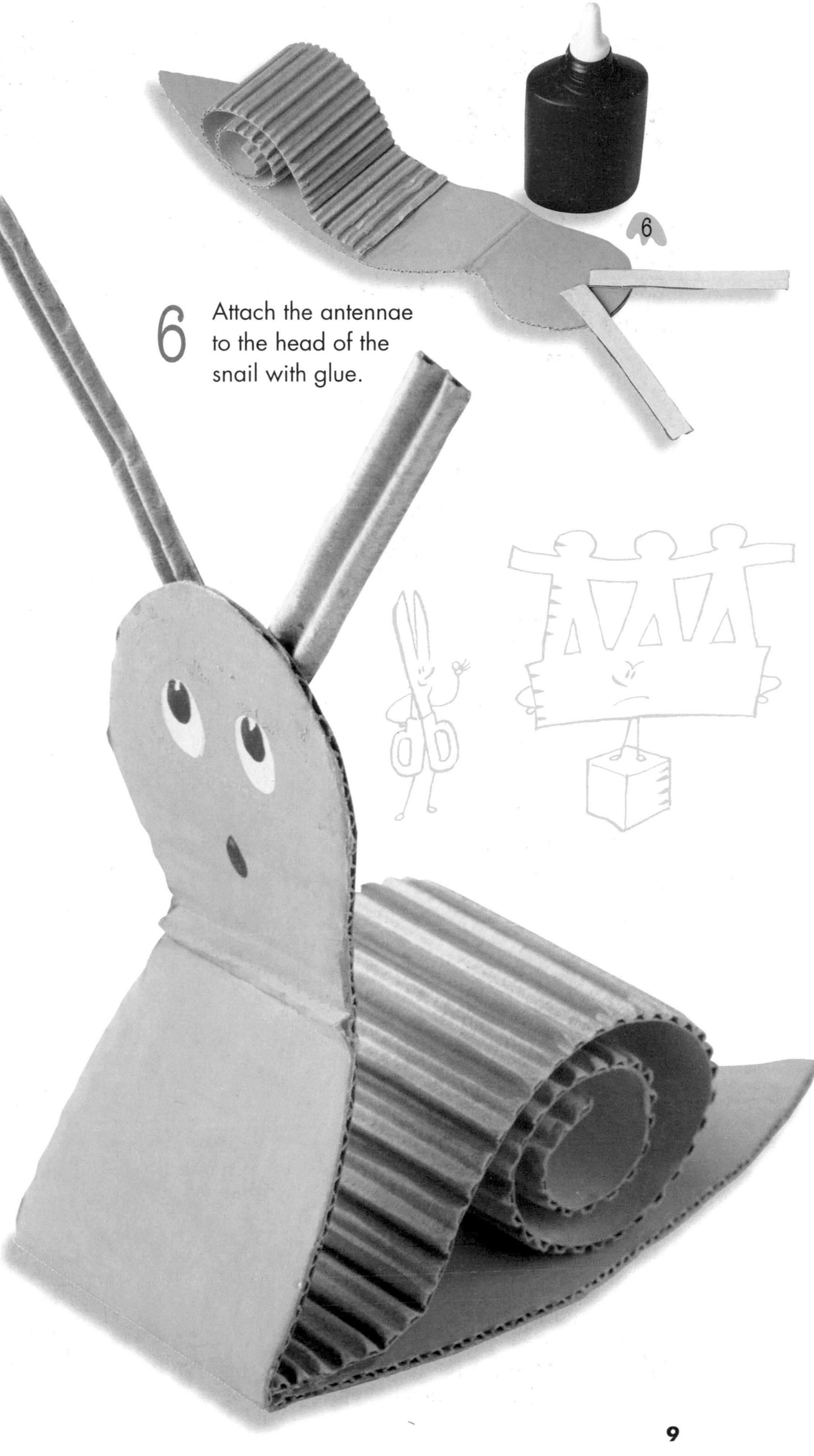

6 Attach the antennae to the head of the snail with glue.

You have finished your new pet! Put it in your room as a decoration.

Let your imagination soar

Other ideas:
Invent other pets that you can make with only two strips of cardboard, like a worm, a snake...

Multistorey Car Park

If you want your cars to be parked better than ever, make a sturdy multistorey car park by following these steps.

1 Draw and cut out three rectangles, each 30 cm by 25 cm, on a piece of thick, smooth cardboard.

2 Make a cut about 20 cm long and 4 cm in from the *short* side of one of the rectangles. Repeat the procedure, but this time on the *long* side of another rectangle. These cuts will make the ramps.

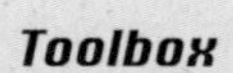

Toolbox

You will need:

- **thin, corrugated cardboard**
- **thick, smooth cardboard**
- **6 toilet tissue tubes**
- **yellow tape**
- **scissors**
- **glue**
- **pink and grey paint**
- **paintbrush**
- **felt-tip pen**

3 Using the rectangle that does not have a ramp as a base, make the two levels of the parking garage using three toilet tissue tubes as columns on each level, and attach them to the rectangles with glue.

4 Finish the edges of the first and second levels with strips of thin corrugated cardboard about 2 cm wide.

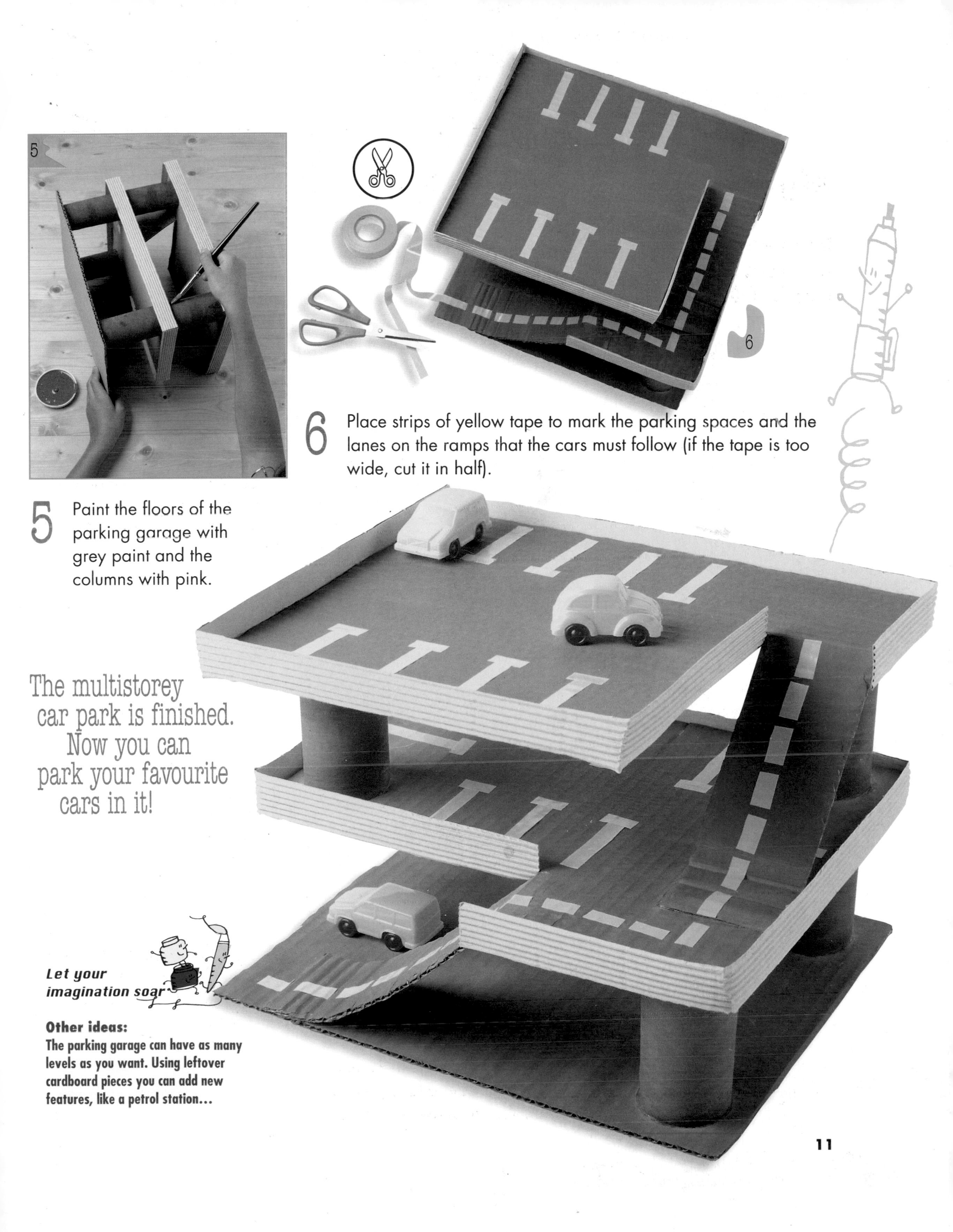

6 Place strips of yellow tape to mark the parking spaces and the lanes on the ramps that the cars must follow (if the tape is too wide, cut it in half).

5 Paint the floors of the parking garage with grey paint and the columns with pink.

The multistorey car park is finished. Now you can park your favourite cars in it!

Let your imagination soar

Other ideas:
The parking garage can have as many levels as you want. Using leftover cardboard pieces you can add new features, like a petrol station...

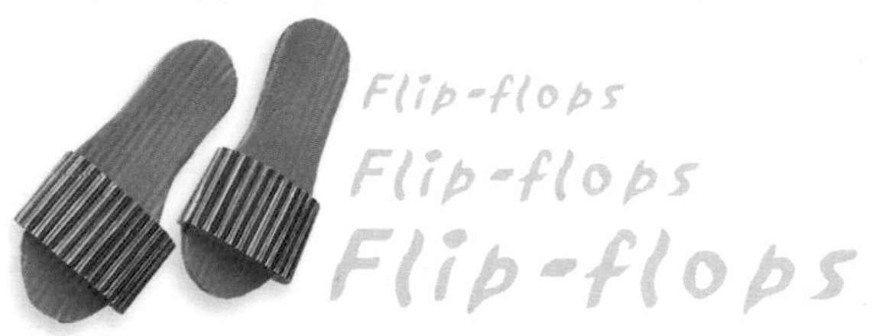

Flip-flops

Do you think you can make a pair of flip-flops? Follow these steps carefully and you will see how easy it is.

Toolbox

You will need:
- thick, smooth cardboard
- thin, corrugated cardboard
- scissors
- glue
- stapler
- white, red and green paint
- paintbrush
- felt-tip pen

1 Trace an outline of the shoe three times on a piece of smooth cardboard. Cut them out.

2 Draw a rectangle about 10 cm long by 6 cm wide on a piece of thin, corrugated cardboard and cut it out.

3 Staple the rectangle to one of the soles that you have cut out.

4 Glue the other two soles, one below and the other one on top of the first one, so that the staples will be concealed.

5 Paint green, red and white stripes on the strip of cardboard.

To make the other flip-flop, follow the same steps. But be careful to copy the outline of the opposite foot! Now you're ready to flip-flop around!

Let your imagination soar

Other ideas:
You can make different designs for the straps on your flip-flops. You can also change the colours.

Camera

Become an expert photographer by making a camera out of a cardboard box. To do it, follow these steps carefully.

Toolbox

You will need:
- **thin, corrugated cardboard**
- **thin, smooth cardboard**
- **thick, smooth cardboard**
- **small square box**
- **toilet tissue tube**
- **scissors**
- **glue**
- **orange, yellow, grey, red and flesh-coloured paint**
- **paintbrush**
- **felt-tip pen**

1 Cut off a piece about 3 cm long from the toilet tissue tube.
This will be the lens.

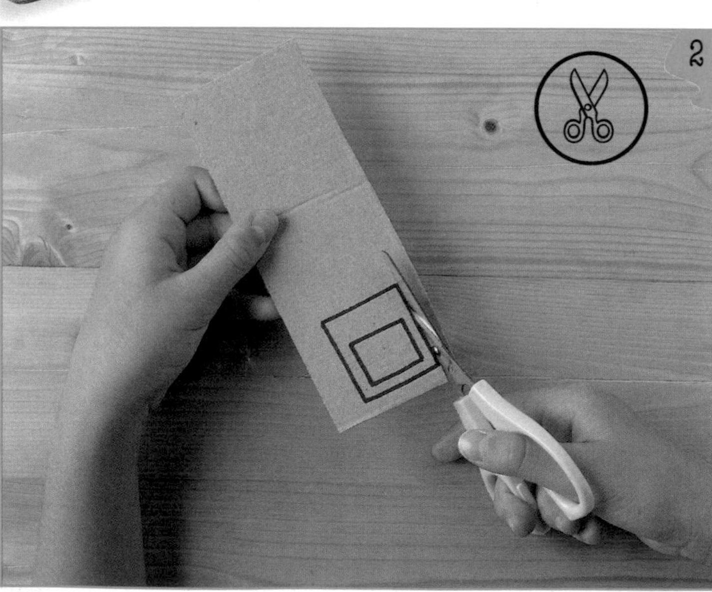

2 Draw a viewer on a piece of thin, smooth cardboard and cut it out.

3 Cut two strips of thin, corrugated cardboard to hang the camera from your neck and glue their smooth sides together.

4 Draw five small circles on a piece of heavy, smooth cardboard, cut them out and glue them all together. They will be the button of the camera.

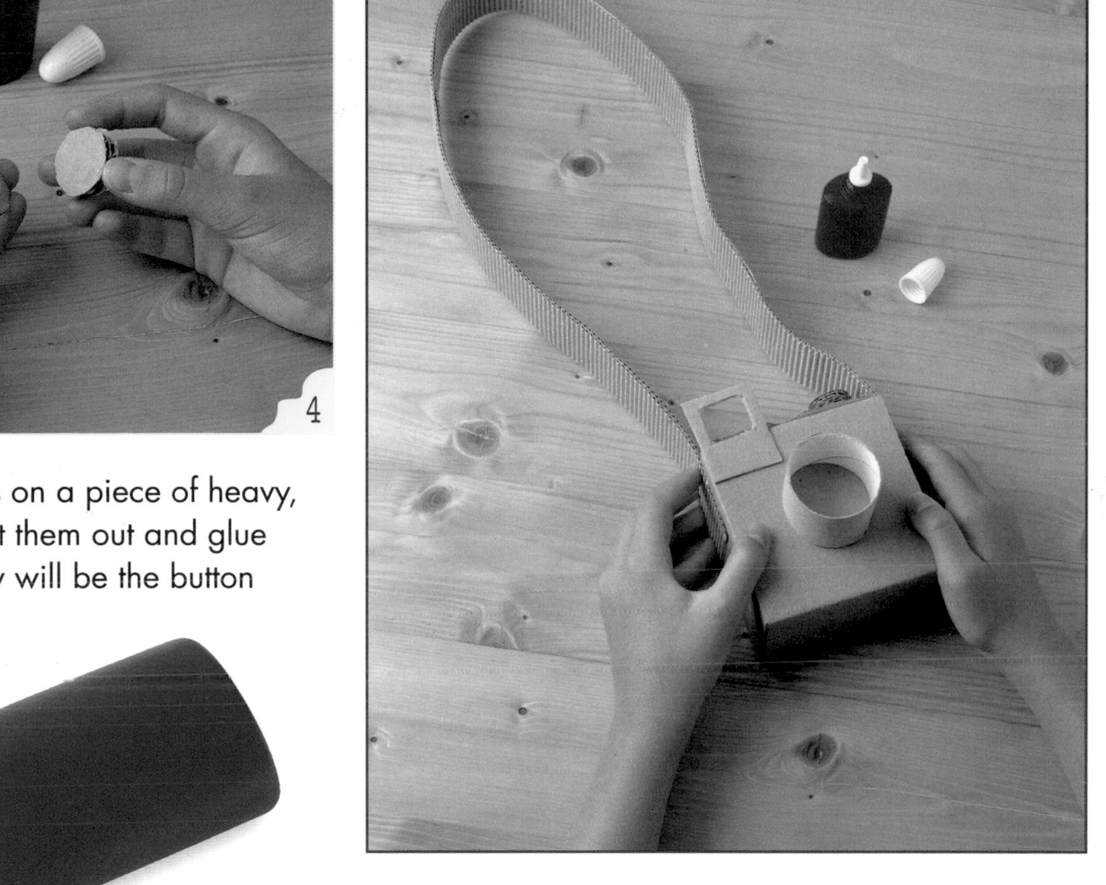

5 Glue all the accessories that you have made onto the square box, as shown here.

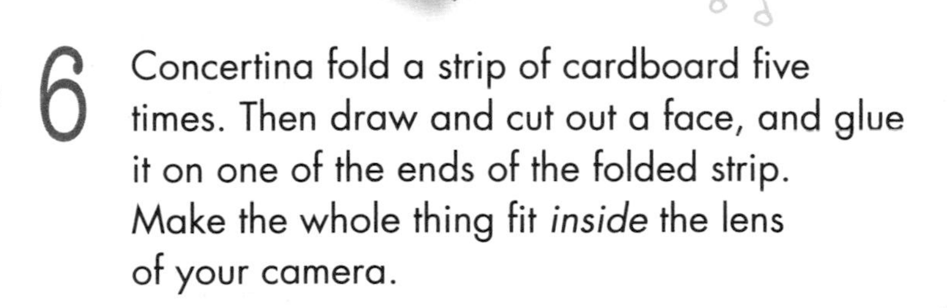

6 Concertina fold a strip of cardboard five times. Then draw and cut out a face, and glue it on one of the ends of the folded strip. Make the whole thing fit *inside* the lens of your camera.

7 Glue the strip with the face inside the lens of the camera.

8 Use the flesh-coloured paint to paint the face, the orange for the hair, black for the eyes and the nose and red for the mouth.

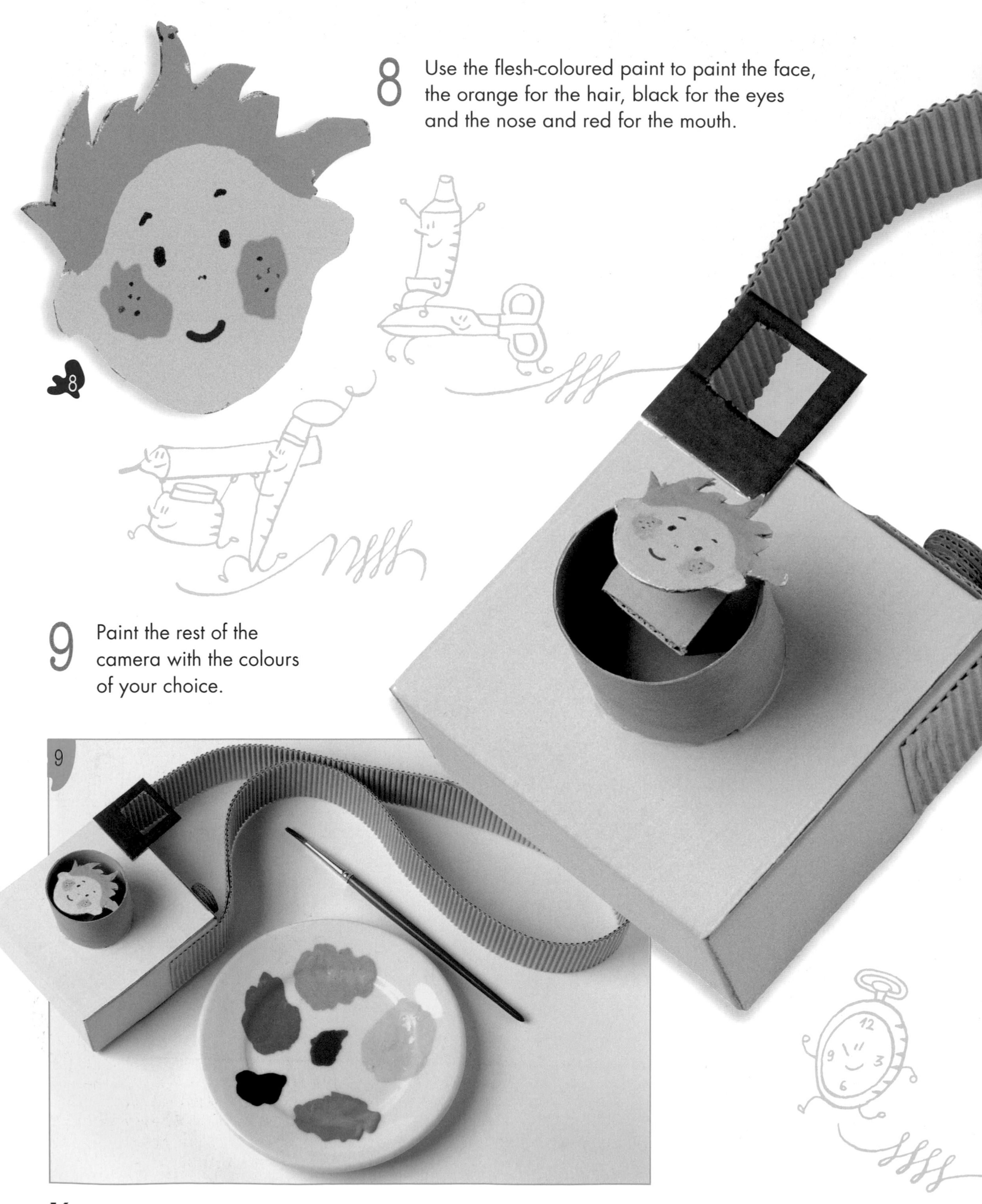

9 Paint the rest of the camera with the colours of your choice.

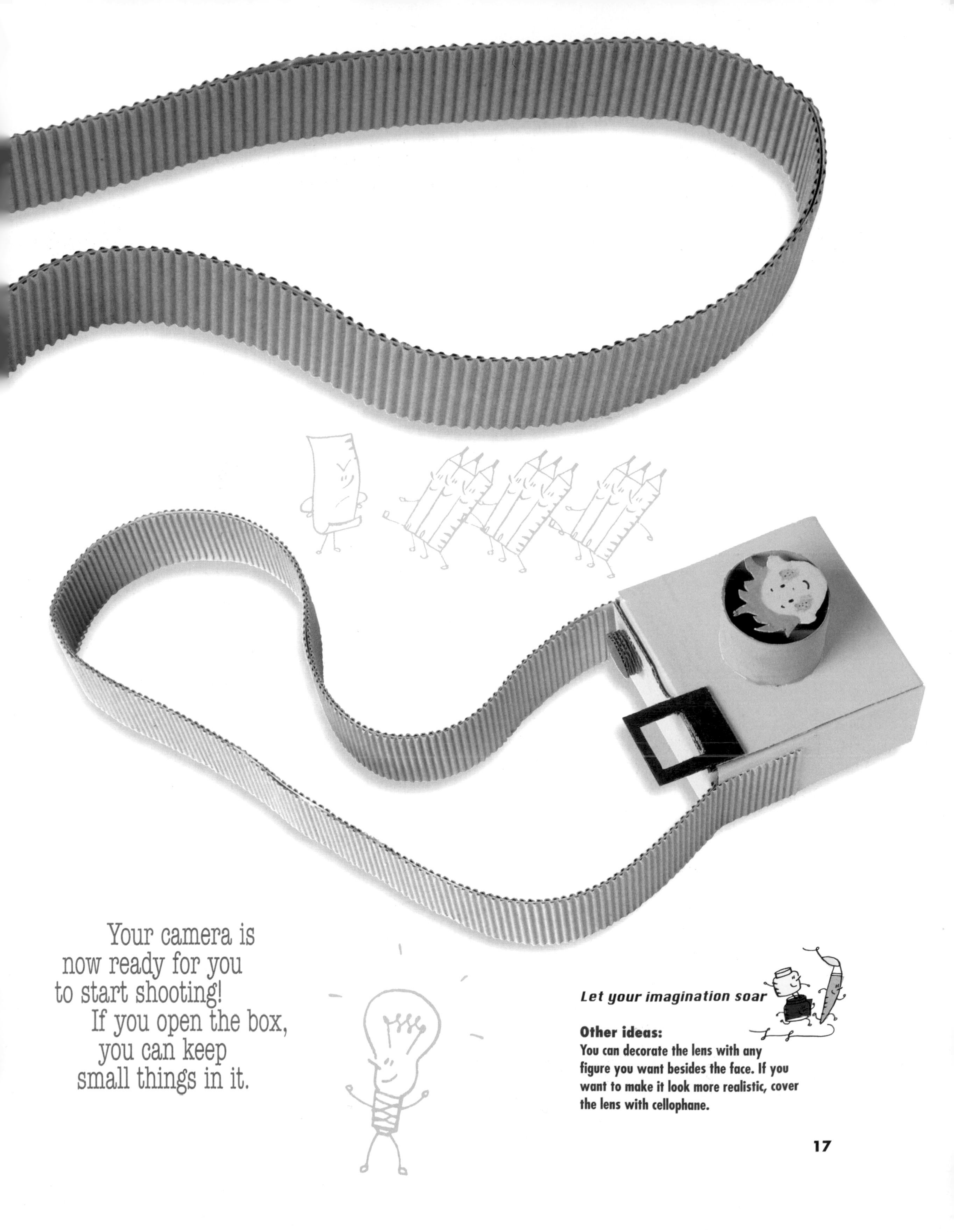

Your camera is now ready for you to start shooting! If you open the box, you can keep small things in it.

Let your imagination soar

Other ideas:
You can decorate the lens with any figure you want besides the face. If you want to make it look more realistic, cover the lens with cellophane.

Hoopla Game

Would you like to make a friendly elephant to play with? If so, follow these steps carefully.

1 Draw a circle on a piece of thick, smooth cardboard using a large plate as a guide and cut it out.

2 Using a smaller plate as a guide, draw and cut out two ears on two other pieces of thick, smooth cardboard.

3 Glue the two ears on the back side of the cut out circle and glue a cardboard tube in the centre.

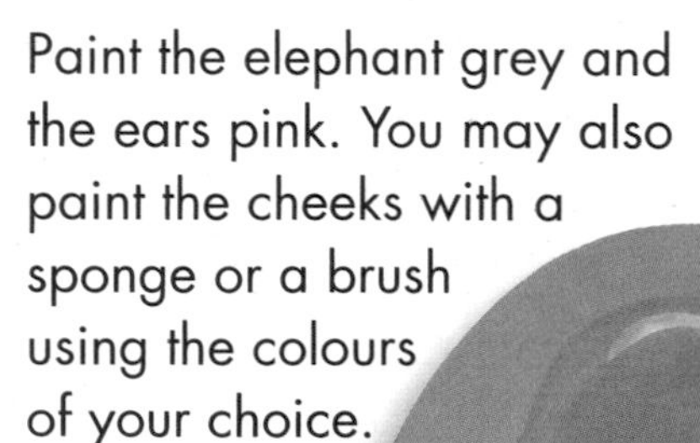

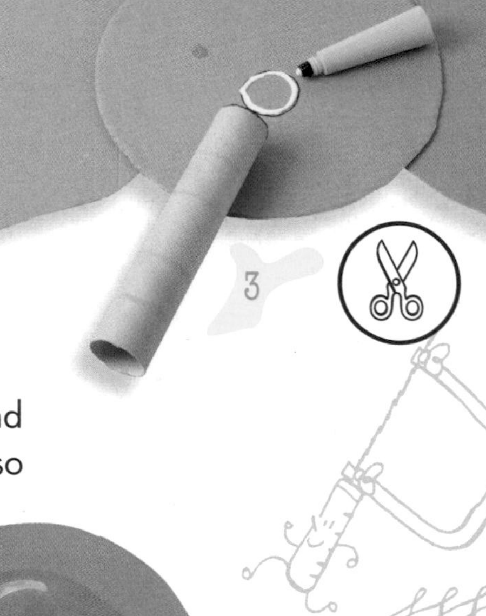

4 Paint the elephant grey and the ears pink. You may also paint the cheeks with a sponge or a brush using the colours of your choice.

Toolbox

You will need:

- thick, smooth cardboard
- thin, smooth cardboard
- paper towel tube
- tape of different colours
- scissors
- glue
- pink, grey, red, orange, white and blue paint
- paintbrush
- felt-tip pen
- compass or different size plates (one small plate, one large)

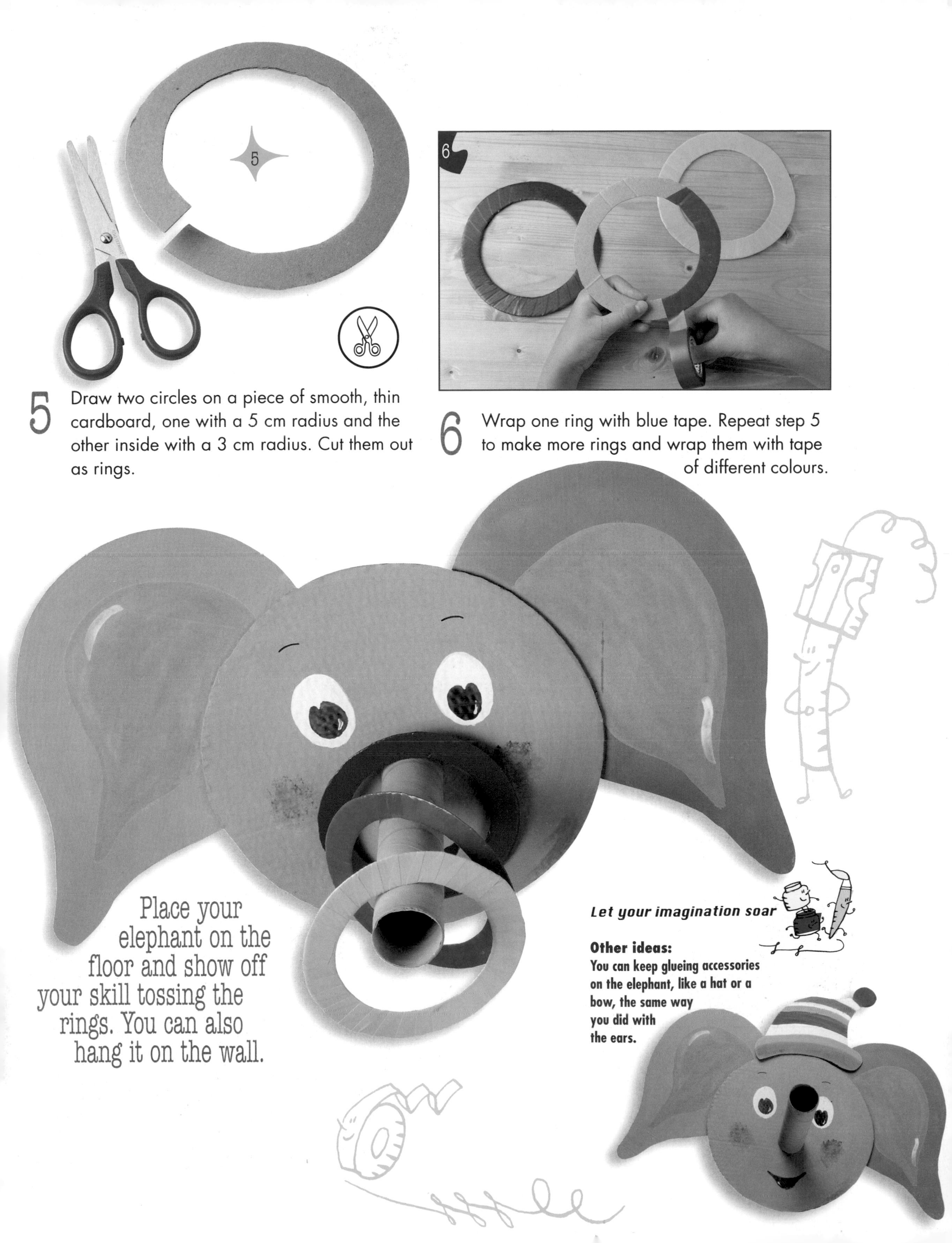

5 Draw two circles on a piece of smooth, thin cardboard, one with a 5 cm radius and the other inside with a 3 cm radius. Cut them out as rings.

6 Wrap one ring with blue tape. Repeat step 5 to make more rings and wrap them with tape of different colours.

Place your elephant on the floor and show off your skill tossing the rings. You can also hang it on the wall.

Let your imagination soar

Other ideas:
You can keep glueing accessories on the elephant, like a hat or a bow, the same way you did with the ears.

Pencil Holder

You can make an original pencil holder with cardboard tubes. To do so you simply have to follow the step-by-step instructions.

1 Make a slit from top to bottom on each of the three toilet tissue tubes.

2 Attach the tubes with staples to make a clover shape.

3 Glue the tubes to a piece of cardboard 12 cm by 12 cm. This will be the base of the pencil holder.

4 When the glue dries, cut the base into a rounded shape with scissors.

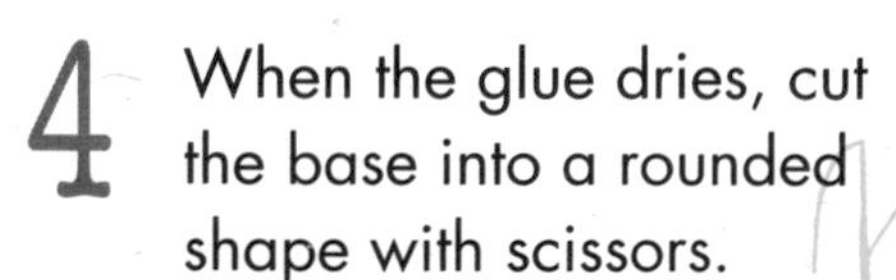

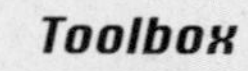

Toolbox

You will need:
- **thick, smooth cardboard**
- **3 toilet tissue tubes**
- **scissors**
- **glue**
- **stapler**
- **paint of different colours**
- **paintbrush**
- **felt-tip pen**

5 Paint the pencil holder with your favourite colours inside and out.

Gather all your coloured pencils and keep them in the holder that you have created.

Let your imagination soar

Other ideas:
You can combine more tubes and make other shapes. You can also decorate your holder with different designs of your choice and change the colours.

Coin Bank Doll

Where can you put your savings? With little more than a cardboard tube, you can rest assured that your savings will be protected. Follow these steps.

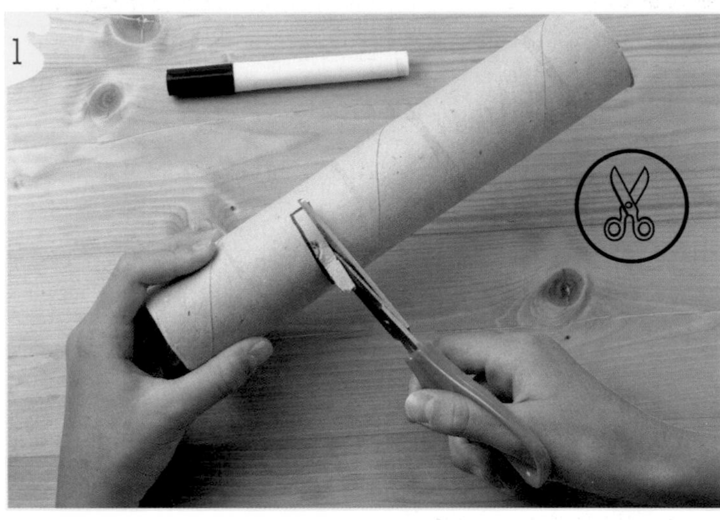

1 Near the top of a cardboard tube (about ⅓ of the way from the top) draw and cut a rectangular slot that will be easy to fit coins through.

2 Colour the tube with blue paint and when it is dry, decorate it with white flowers.

Toolbox

You will need:

- thin, corrugated cardboard
- thick, smooth cardboard
- thin, smooth cardboard
- 2 paper towel tubes
- scissors
- glue
- white, blue, red, green and yellow paint
- paintbrush
- felt-tip pen

3 Draw and cut out the shape of a face on a piece of thin, smooth cardboard. Also draw and cut out feet (from a piece of thick cardboard).

5 Cut a piece about 3 cm wide from the other tube to make the lid of the coin bank. Roll a strip of thin, corrugated cardboard so that it will fit into the tube you have just cut out, and glue it to the inside.

4 Colour the feet and the face of the doll with paints of different colours.

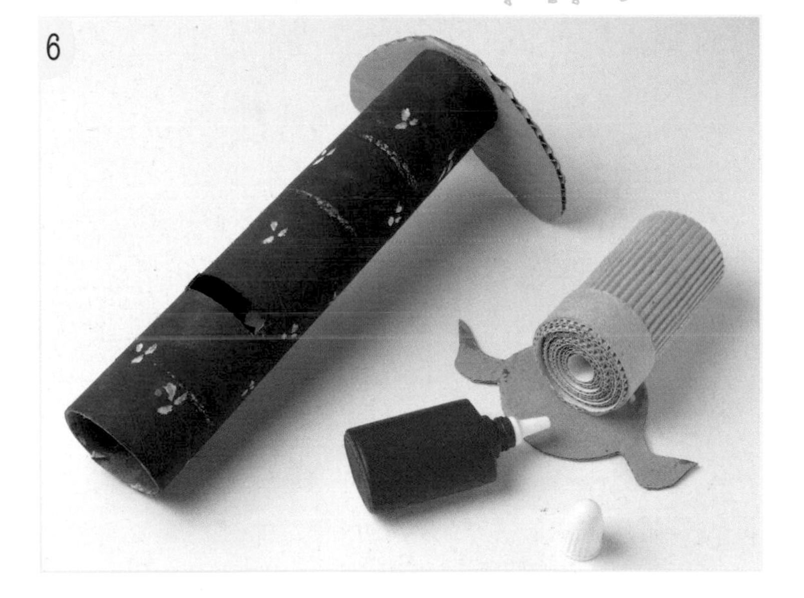

6 Glue the feet of the doll to the base of the painted tube and the face to the lid of the coin bank.

Let your imaginations soar

Other ideas:
You can change the face and turn your bank into an animal, such as a cat.

Now all you have to do is put the lid on the coin bank. This doll can help you save a lot of money.

Drawers

Toolbox

You will need:
- thin, smooth cardboard
- 2 boxes
- scissors
- glue
- green, orange and blue paint
- paintbrush
- felt-tip pen
- ruler

Where do you keep your things? You can make yourself some drawers by following these steps.

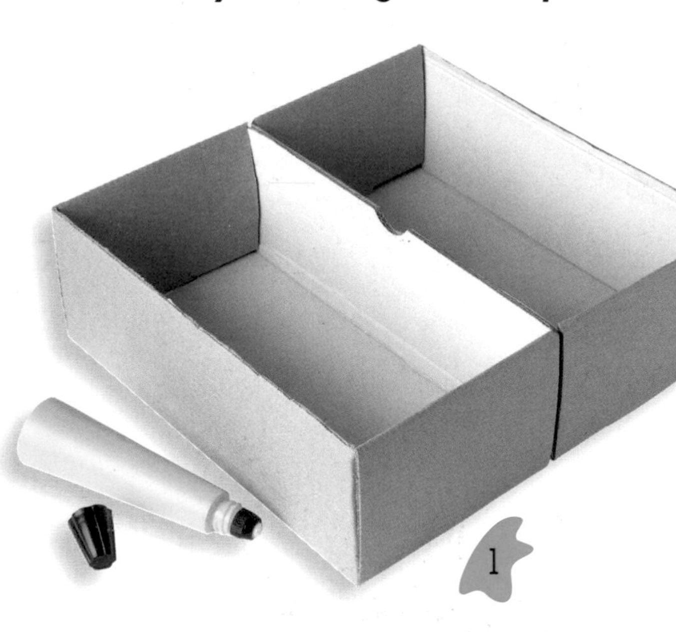

1 Glue two boxes of the same size side by side.

2 With the help of an adult, draw three open boxes on a piece of cardboard. One of them should be slightly smaller than each of the boxes already put together. The other two should be half as large. Remember to draw tabs for assembling the boxes.

3 After you cut them out, fold them along the lines and glue them together.

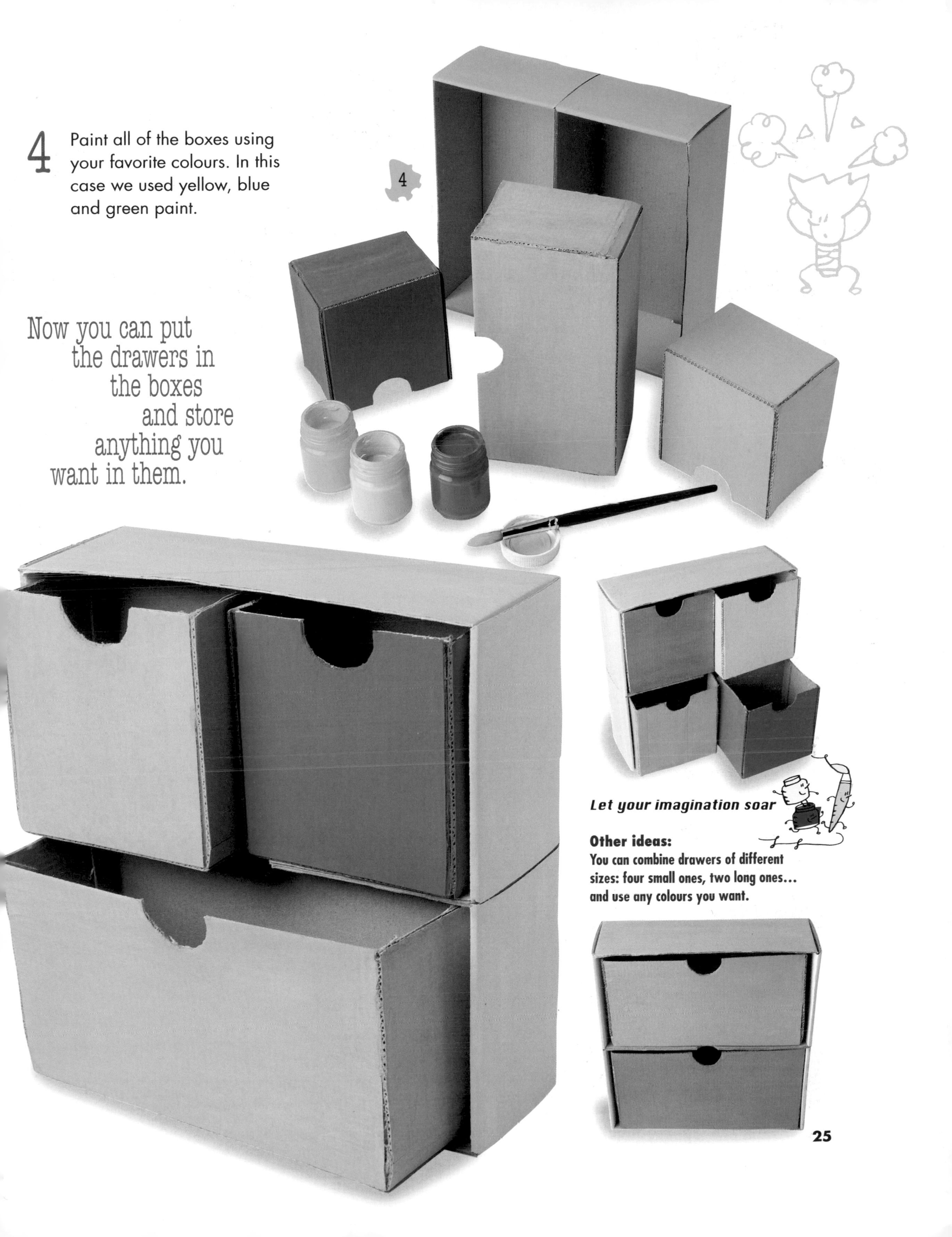

4 Paint all of the boxes using your favorite colours. In this case we used yellow, blue and green paint.

Now you can put the drawers in the boxes and store anything you want in them.

Let your imagination soar

Other ideas:
You can combine drawers of different sizes: four small ones, two long ones... and use any colours you want.

Balancing Parrot
Balancing Parrot

Balancing Parrot

Toolbox

You will need:
- thin, smooth cardboard
- scissors
- glue
- green and other coloured paints
- paintbrush
- felt-tip pen
- modelling clay

Do you think you can make a parrot that can hang onto a shelf and even dance on it? In order for your parrot to become an acrobat follow these steps carefully.

1 Draw the body of the parrot on a piece of thin, smooth cardboard and cut it out.

2 Draw and cut out two wings from a different piece of the same cardboard.

3 Glue the wings to the body of the parrot, one on each side.

4 Paint the parrot green, placing it on a piece of cardboard to prevent the table from getting dirty.

5 Paint the feathers, the beak and the eyes of the parrot with different colours.

6 Attach enough modelling clay to the tail of the parrot to keep it balanced on a shelf when hanging by its beak.

Have you been able to balance your parrot? If not, add or take away modelling clay until you can do it.

Let your imagination soar

Other ideas:
You can make other balancing animals or figures, for example, a monkey, a clown...

Scissors Case

Make a case and put your scissors in it so they do not hurt anybody by accident. You can make it by following these simple steps.

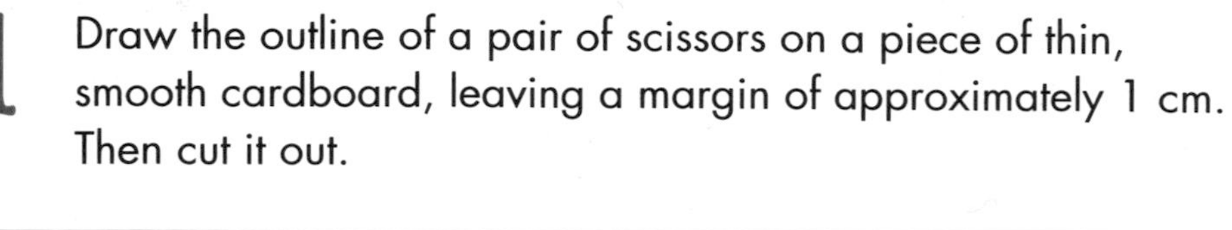

1 Draw the outline of a pair of scissors on a piece of thin, smooth cardboard, leaving a margin of approximately 1 cm. Then cut it out.

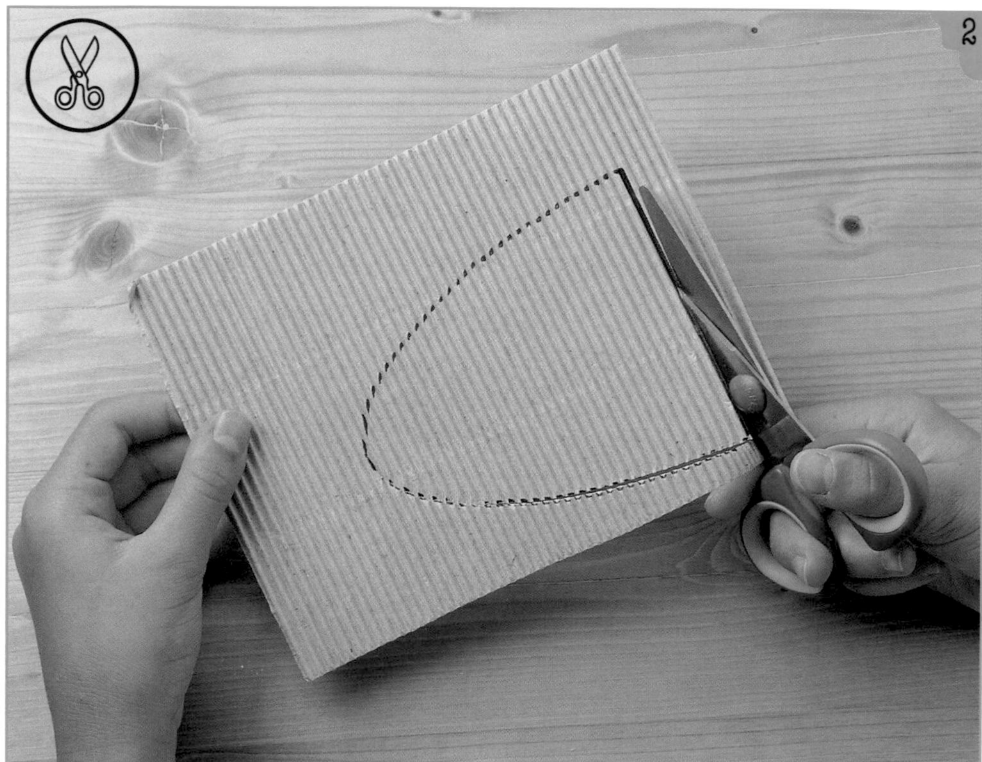

Toolbox

You will need:
- thin, smooth cardboard
- thin, corrugated cardboard
- scissors
- stapler
- pink, red, white, green and black paint
- paintbrush
- felt-tip pen

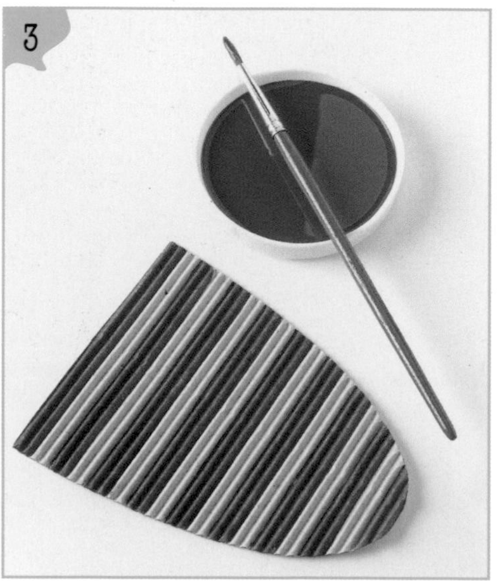

2 Use the piece you just cut out to trace the pocket for your case. Keep in mind that the pocket should be shorter so the scissors stick out.

3 Paint pink stripes on the pocket piece of thin, corrugated cardboard.

4

Staple both pieces of cardboard together and paint a pair of eyes and a nose on the back piece.

When the paint is dry, you can put the scissors inside the case.

Let your imagination soar

Other ideas:

You can make a larger case to keep other things in. You can also change the colours.

Picture Frame

Would you like to frame your favourite picture? You can make your own frame. Simply follow these steps.

Toolbox

You will need:

- thin corrugated cardboard
- thin, smooth cardboard
- thick, smooth cardboard
- scissors
- glue
- pink paint
- paintbrush
- felt-tip pen
- ruler
- tweezers
- clothes pegs

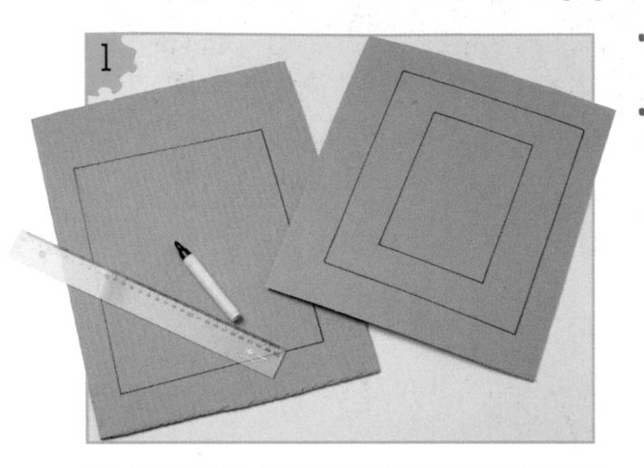

1 Draw a 20 cm by 25 cm rectangle on a piece of thick cardboard. Do the same on a thin, smooth piece and draw a rectangle inside it a little smaller than the picture you want to frame.

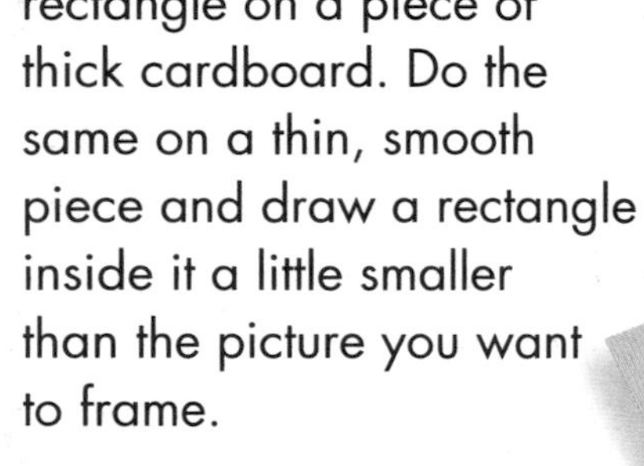

2 Cut out the rectangles, including the one you have drawn inside, to turn it into a frame.

3 Glue the frame to the thick, smooth cardboard rectangle, leaving one of its sides open.

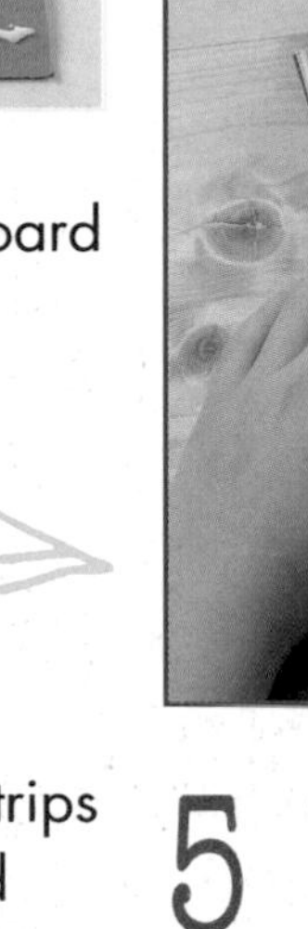

4 Cut two 20 cm strips of the corrugated cardboard and two more 50 cm long.

5 Glue the strips of corrugated cardboard around the frame. Form wavy shapes on the two longer sides holding them in place with clothes pegs until the glue dries.

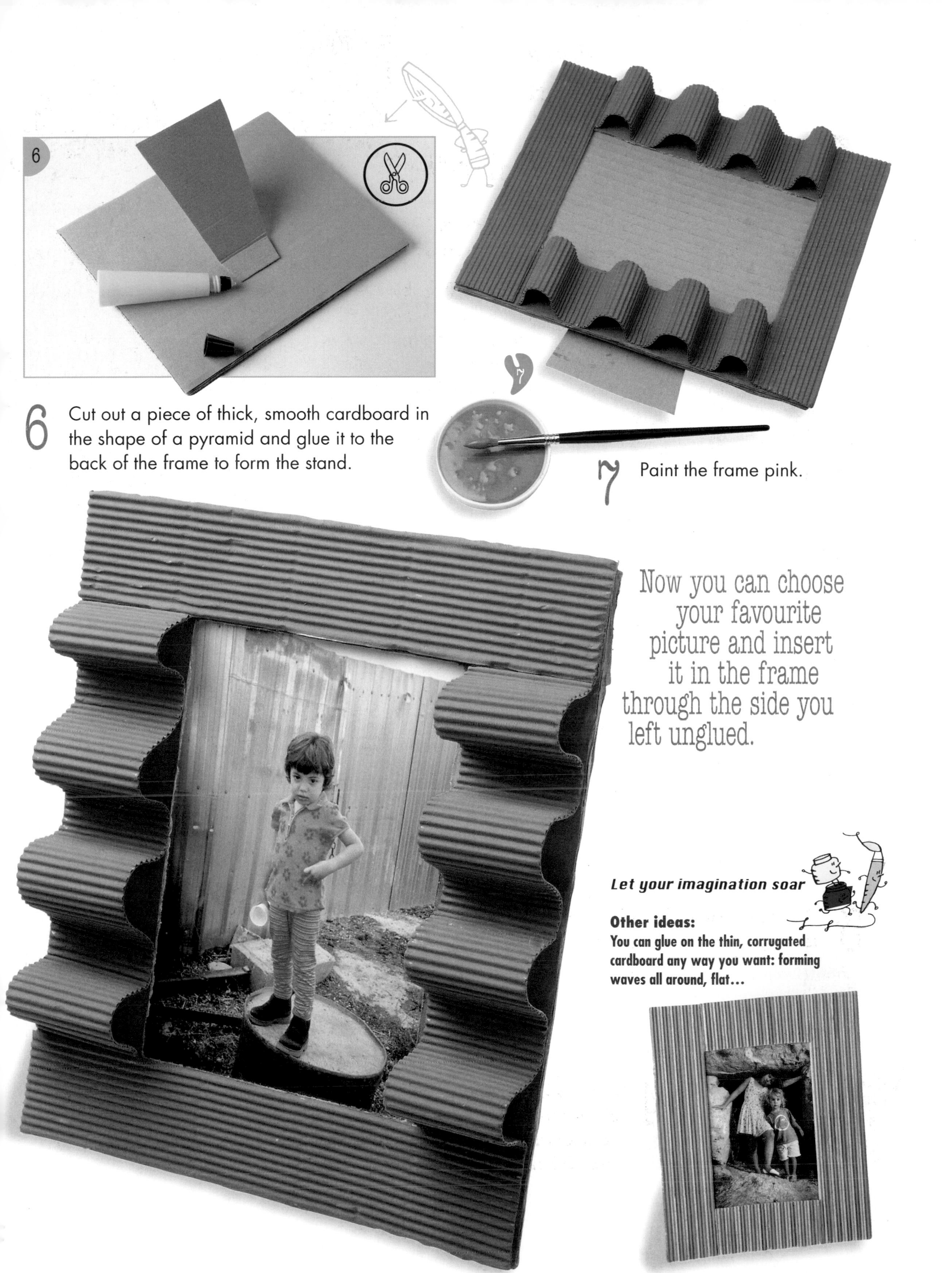

6 Cut out a piece of thick, smooth cardboard in the shape of a pyramid and glue it to the back of the frame to form the stand.

7 Paint the frame pink.

Now you can choose your favourite picture and insert it in the frame through the side you left unglued.

Let your imagination soar

Other ideas:
You can glue on the thin, corrugated cardboard any way you want: forming waves all around, flat...

Make it with 

Cardboard

Notes for parents and teachers

Cardboard is a very appropriate material for craft projects, due to the great number of possibilities that it offers. It can be cut, glued and painted easily with items found at home. It is important to stress the idea of using everyday things as a basis for making the various projects. This way the child will have the materials to create things at home as well as at school.

Following are some suggestions for making each project, as well as a guide to the most appropriate age level of each one. It is important to point out that the suggested age is based on the degree of difficulty of the process, but the projects can be easily adapted to varying age levels.

p.6 **Table-tennis Paddle.** It is important for each child to make his or her own paddle, to invent a new shape or to decorate it with original motifs.
Ages 6 and up

p.8 **Snail.** To make the project more interesting, snails of different sizes can be made, which can be put together in a mobile.
Ages 5 and up

p.10 **Multistorey Car Park.** Various materials can be used to decorate the car park. Different coloured contact paper can be used to decorate it or it can be covered with magazine cut-outs using the *collage* technique.
Ages 7 and up

p.12 **Flip-flops.** To make these more durable, a piece of fabric can be used as a substitute for the light, corrugated cardboard, following the same steps.
Ages 6 and up

p.14 **Camera.** It can also be coloured with wax crayons and later painted with a coat of latex varnish.
Ages 7 and up

p.18 **Ring Toss Game.** One elephant can be made for the class and each child can make his or her own ring.
Ages 6 and up

p.20 **Pencil Holder.** It is a good idea for the child to invent the shape of the base of the holder, trying it out first with pencil on paper, so it can also be used as a template.
Ages 5 and up

p.22 **Coin Bank Doll.** It is important for the child to decorate the money bank his or her own way, using the accessories of his or her choice (arms, fabric for covering the tube...)
Ages 6 and up

p.24 **Drawers.** If an adult makes the templates for the drawers this project can also be recommended for children ages 6 and up.
Ages 8 and up

p.26 **Balancing Parrot.** Once the parrot is finished, the child, without the help of an adult, should try to balance it, by adding or removing the modelling clay.
Ages 5 and up

p.28 **Case for Scissors.** This craft can be made at the beginning of the school year so the children can use the case to keep their scissors in throughout the entire year. This way they will realise that they can create useful objects.
Ages 5 and up

p.30 **Frame.** Following the same steps the children may also frame a drawing made by themselves.
Ages 6 and up